A Thousand Dirty Buckets:

Finding Fulfillment in the Most Unlikely Place

By Bob Franquiz

Cover Design by Mark Rodriguez
Interior Design by Gus Beltrami
Back Cover Photo by Mark Rodriguez
Printed in the United States of America

To the faithful servants who make Calvary Fellowship a place where God is glorified, lost people are found, and believers are discipled.

TABLE OF CONTENTS

INTRODUCTION

Down is the New Up

My day started at 6 AM. My role? Brew coffee for 200 hundred people, set up chairs for eight classes and cut fruit and bagels for those that would attend. That was my introduction into service. I was nineteen years old and I had only been a Christian for a year, but even then I knew I was involved in holy work. The question you're asking is, "What's so holy about brewing coffee?" With all due respect to baristas everywhere, there's nothing inherently special about the act of brewing coffee or setting up chairs. Yet what makes this act an act of worship is the Person to which these actions are directed. Serving, in whatever shape or form it takes is worship. Yet somehow, the act of worship got lost in the shuffle. Today when we mention worship, our minds think about the first 20 minutes of a church service. This book is my way of trying to fix that problem.

This book started out as a tiny pamphlet that I wrote for those in my church who desired to serve. Yet as I began writing, there was so much I wanted to say that the pamphlet grew beyond a few pages and became a few chapters. So I knew that either this book needed to go on a diet or I could allow God to shape its direction.

This book comes out of a passion for the church. Today, it seems as though it's in vogue to speak ill of the church and complain about what the church isn't doing, but I want to tell you up front that I love the Church. The Church is the Bride of Christ and it's never a good idea to talk bad about someone's wife, especially when that Person is Jesus.

Honestly, when I thought about giving a book to the new servants who were joining our team at Calvary Fellowship, I looked for a book to buy, not to write. Yet as I searched bookstores and online retailers, I couldn't find a book that said what I felt needed to be communicated to a new generation of servants that are sticking their toes in the waters of service. I found many books

> **"I pray this book lifts us out of our seats and into the game."**

about discovering your gifts, which is vitally important. I read books about the importance of volunteering, which I also affirm. Yet I did not find a book that succinctly dealt with the subject of servanthood. One of the books that changed my life was "On Being a Servant of God" by Warren Wiersbe. In this petite powder keg, Wiersbe reminds Pastors that above all, we are servants. This book changed how I viewed the position of Pastor and is a book that I keep within an arm's length of my desk because its wisdom has continued to speak to me over the years.

My desire is that "A Thousand Dirty Buckets" can stir up in a new generation of servants what "On Being a Servant of God" did for me as a twenty-year-old kid wanting to serve God in the ministry. I pray this book lifts us out of our seats and into the game. My hope is that what you find within these pages will inspire you to step out and serve God in whatever capacity He makes available to you. Chuck Smith, one of the men I most respect said that "God doesn't call the equipped; He equips the called." As a Christian, you are part of the priesthood of all believers and you get to participate in the service of the king.

So why call a book about servanthood "A Thousand Dirty Buckets"? It is because as a Pastor my desire is to engage every believer who calls my church home to serve the Lord in some form or fashion. So my mind began to wander and I thought, "What would our community look like if everyone in our church rolled up their sleeves and grabbed a towel and a bucket in the spirit of John 13 and served others?" I think we can agree that our cities would never be the same.

> **What would our community look like if everyone in our church rolled up their sleeves and grabbed a towel and a bucket in the spirit of John 13 and served others? I think we can agree that our cities would never be the same.**

There's another reason I gave this book its title. We tend to think of a bucket and a mop as the bottom rung on the ladder to greatness and success. Yet Jesus teaches us that the bucket (service) is the way to achieve greatness.

"But he who is greatest among you shall be your servant." **(Matthew 23:11)**

When I talk about serving, I'm not just talking about volunteering your time. There's a difference between volunteering and servanthood.

> **Greatness is not the amount of people who serve you; it's the amount of people you serve out of obedience to Jesus.**

Volunteering simply means freely giving your time. I'm grateful for the volunteers who give of themselves for the sake of many worthwhile causes. Servanthood is different from volunteering because servanthood involves a calling and a commissioning from our Savior. When we serve the Lord, we are involved in holy work. It might look simple (like setting up chairs or singing a song), but when it's done in the name of the Lord, it's sanctified and set apart for a special purpose.

So the real question is, "Do you want to be great?" If so, the way to the top is to grab a towel and a bucket and serve. In our culture, we are experiencing an identity crisis. The reason? Too many believe that life is about achieving a certain status where people "serve us." However, Jesus said life is about "service." Greatness is not the amount of people who serve you; it's the amount of people you serve out of obedience to Jesus. So let's fill up our buckets and begin…

CHAPTER ONE

Identity Theft

"I find the whole mythology surrounding superheroes fascinating.
Take my favorite superhero, Superman. Not a great comic book.
Not particularly well-drawn. But the mythology...The mythology is not
only great, it's unique. Now, a staple of the superhero mythology is,
there's the superhero and there's the alter ego. Batman is actually
Bruce Wayne; Spider-Man is actually Peter Parker. When that character
wakes up in the morning, he's Peter Parker. He has to put on a costume
to become Spider-Man. And it is in that characteristic Superman stands
alone. Superman didn't become Superman. Superman was born Superman.
When Superman wakes up in the morning, he's Superman. His alter ego
is Clark Kent. His outfit with the big red "S" - that's the blanket he was
wrapped in as a baby when the Kents found him. Those are his clothes.
What Kent wears - the glasses, the business suit - that's the costume.
That's the costume Superman wears to blend in with us. Clark Kent is
how Superman views us. And what are the characteristics of
Clark Kent? He's weak...he's unsure of himself...he's a coward.
Clark Kent is Superman's critique on the whole human race."

- Bill (Kill Bill Volume II)

I was picking up a few items at a local supermarket. After swiping my debit card to pay for the goodies in my cart, the machine declined my card. Anyone who has experienced this knows how embarrassing this scenario can be. I was mortified. What made matters worse is that I knew I had enough money in the account to pay for $40 worth of groceries! But for some reason I was declined. Just a few doors down in the same strip mall was the bank in which I had opened my checking account, so I went up to the ATM machine and checked my balance. What I saw nearly caused me to grab my chest and started calling out to Elizabeth a la Fred Sanford because this was "The big one!" The bank said I was $1,000 overdrawn! So I went home in a panic and called the bank. I got on the phone with a "personal banking specialist" and shared my story with them. Then she started asking me some very odd questions. She asked, "Mr. Franquiz, have you been to Las Vegas recently?" I said, "Miss, I have never been to Las Vegas in my life." Then she asked, "So why was your card used at Caesar's Palace over the weekend?" I said, "That's why I'm calling you! My account is overdrawn and that can't be possible!" At that moment we both realized what had happened. I had been the victim of identity theft. At some point in time, my debit card number was stolen and someone decided to have a vacation at my expense! I may sound crazy, but if anyone is going to have a vacation at my expense it should be me!

Think about what identity theft is. It is a person acting as though they are someone else. It creates a world where the thief has access to places where he would normally not be able to go and takes money he would normally never have. Quite simply, he is an impersonator. They act like someone else and use someone else's name to exact what they want.

Yet there's an identity we have as followers of Jesus. It is an identity that every Christian gets to have, and it's better than any other identification we have because it reflects our relationship with God. And this is the one that Jesus Himself committed identity theft to get. Think about that for a moment: Jesus committing identity theft. Yet isn't that what the incarnation is? I understand that calling it identity theft makes is sound illegal, so why don't we call it, "Identity borrowing?" Jesus took on human flesh to enter the world as a man and die for our sins, but also to give us a picture of a life completely submitted to God. There are many things that Jesus is: Son of God, King of Kings, Lord over All, Wonderful, Counselor, Prince of Peace, Alpha and Omega, The beginning and the End. The list is endless. However, the one thing He didn't have to be was a servant. An earthly king doesn't have to take a lesser role, much less the king of heaven! Yet He did, to show us what our real identity is.

"Let this mind be in you which was also in Christ Jesus, who, being in the form of God, did not consider it robbery to be equal with God, but made Himself of no reputation, taking the form of a bondservant, and coming in the likeness of men. And being found in appearance as a man, He humbled Himself and became obedient to the point of death, even the death of the cross." **(Philippians 2:5-8 NKJV)**

FAKE I.D.

As is quoted above, the idea of Superman becoming Clark Kent can't even begin to compare to the kind of identity transformation that the Son of God took on to come to earth in our likeness. The fictional character, Bill, believed that Clark Kent was Superman's commentary on mankind, believing that humanity was clumsy, weak, and cowardly. Yet the original Super-Man, Jesus, took on human flesh to show humanity everything we could be. He came and died a brutal death on the cross to set Mankind free of the sin in which we wallowed and allows us now to not merely exist, but live an abundant life. In order to do this, there would need to be the exchanging of one identity for another. This is not to imply that Jesus was not fully God

" Yet the original Super-Man, Jesus, took on human flesh to show humanity everything we could be. "

when He came to earth, Instead, it is to say that Jesus emptied Himself to some degree to become human (God is omnipresent, for example, yet Jesus limited Himself to His physical body while here on earth). What Jesus also knew was that serving God and having the heart of a servant was the best possible way to live. Yet I wonder if that is what the disciples of Jesus were thinking during the last Passover meal they were sharing with Him? Jesus had spoken to them about His suffering, His death, and His resurrection. He instituted the Lord's Supper and revealed who His betrayer would be. But He waited for the end of the evening to unveil His greatest lesson. Jesus Christ, the Son of God, committed identity theft! He took on someone else's identity, someone else's role, so He could do what they were required to do. In doing so, He modeled for us the kind of heart that every disciple of Jesus should have beating in his chest.

" He modeled for us the kind of heart that every disciple of Jesus should have beating in his chest. "

"Before the Passover celebration, Jesus knew that his hour had come to leave this world and return to his Father. He now showed the disciples the full extent of his love. It was time for supper, and the Devil had already enticed Judas, son of Simon Iscariot, to carry out his plan to betray Jesus. Jesus knew that the Father had given him authority over everything and that he had come from God and would return to God. So he got up from the table, took off his robe, wrapped a towel around his waist, and poured water into a basin. Then he began to wash the disciples' feet and to wipe them with the towel he had around him." **(John 13:1-5NLT)**

A TABLE FOR THIRTEEN

I'm going to make an assumption here and believe that if you're reading this book, you have seen a painting of DiVinci's Last Supper (If you haven't, Google it. I'll be here when you get back). You have to understand that this painting, while beautiful, is completely inaccurate as to what the Last Supper would have looked like. These men were celebrating a Passover meal, and being Jewish, they would have been seated the way Jewish men in the first century sat. Besides, who sits all on one side of the table? That's just weird! Couples who do that in restaurants drive me crazy, so could you imagine a group of men going to Outback and saying, "We'd like a table for thirteen, but we're all going to sit on one side?" Instead, they sat around the table. In the Jewish custom, they would actually be laying because the table was only a foot or so off the ground. The table was three-sided (imagine a table that's U-shaped). Jesus would be sitting second to the end, which is the spot the host would sit in. The first spot (to the right of Jesus is where John the apostle is sitting (remember he leaned on Jesus' chest? That's how he would talk to Jesus because Jesus was practically behind him). On Jesus' left is Judas (In the place of honor). [1] We know this because he dips his bread with Jesus and no one thinks anything

1 – Alfred Edersheim The Life and Time of Jesus the Messiah (Hendrickson Publishers, Inc. Peabody, MA 1993) Pg. 815

of it. We're not really sure where everyone else was sitting, except for Peter. Peter was in the last spot, across from John on the other side of the U-shaped table. There's nothing wrong with this spot except that this is the place where the servants would sit. The person sitting there was supposed to wash everyone's feet as they came in. Now we don't know why Peter got stuck sitting here. Maybe he got there late, or maybe he lost he some ancient form of "Rock, Paper, Scissors"; either way he ended up in the last seat. Since Peter didn't do the job of the servant, Jesus, who was seated in the place of honor got up, put on a towel (Think: apron), got on His knees and washed their feet. Understand, people in those days wore sandals and even when they bathed, their feet would still get dirty. So it was customary for a servant to wash the feet of a guest to make them feel refreshed, relaxed, and welcomed. So why is Jesus doing this act that should be done by some "other" person? First, no one else would do it. Secondly, according to Luke's Gospel, they had just finished having an argument during their meal over who was the greatest (Luke 22:24-30). To humble oneself within this group was to say that you really weren't the greatest. Yet Jesus has been trying to get through to them over and over that the secret to greatness is servanthood. So He washes their feet and after an exchange with Peter, says this...

> **"Yet Jesus has been trying to get through to them over and over that the secret to greatness is servanthood."**

"After washing their feet, he put on his robe again and sat down and asked, "Do you understand what I was doing? You call me `Teacher' and `Lord,' and you are right, because it is true. And since I, the Lord and Teacher, have washed your feet, you ought to wash each other's feet. I have given you an example to follow. Do as I have done to you. How true it is that a servant is not greater than the master. Nor are messengers more important than the one who sends them. You know these things--now do them! That is the path of blessing." **(John 13:12-17NLT)**

> **If we are going to reach our full potential as believers in Jesus, we must follow the example of the One who showed what it is to truly be human.**

Jesus decided to take on the identity of a servant. The only Person who did not need to take on this distinctive is the very one who made it His own. Why? It's because the identity He took on was ours. The role He was modeling was the one that was created for you and me. The issue isn't that we simply know this. Jesus said we are blessed if we do them. So I invite you on the journey of learning the blessing of what it means to serve God by serving others. If we are going to reach our full potential as believers in Jesus, we must follow the example of the One who showed what it is to truly be human. We must look in the mirror and see if we are reflecting the likeness of the One whose image we bear...

CHAPTER TWO

Body Piercing

"Today I saw a slave become more powerful than the Emperor of Rome."
- **Lucilla (Gladiator)**

My parents only spoke to me in Spanish, so they put me in preschool to learn English and start kindergarten without needing an interpreter. I do remember my first English memory: I was four years old. It was 1977 and Star wars had been released and was taking the world (or should I say, galaxy) by storm. I was still learning English so I didn't have much of a vocabulary yet, but I remember a kid in my class saying to me, "Let's play Star Wars. I'll be Darth Vader, you can be a Storm Trooper, OK?" I didn't know who The Dark Lord of the Sith was or what a storm trooper was, but I said, "OK (Add slight Spanish accent for affect)." I was reminded of this recently because my nephew James is totally obsessed with Star Wars. His cousin brought over his Darth Vader helmet recently and two light sabers and fought each other for two hours. My brother-in-law and I just watched and made commentary (Picture

Mystery Science Theatre 3000. We were the dudes in the front row). Every once in a while, James would pull off the helmet and say, "I am Darth Vader." Then he would put the helmet on and the battle between good and evil would commence.

James reminded me of something that is important to all of us. Kids want to be someone in the story. They want to be the good guy; they are even OK with being the bad guy, if they get to wear the Darth Vader helmet. But don't ask a kid to be a storm trooper, because trust me, he won't want to be one. Anyway, back to 1977. I played Star Wars that day as a Storm Trooper. But after I found out what a Storm Trooper was, I felt used and cheated. I don't care if I'm Luke Skywalker, Obi-Wan Kenobi, Darth Vader, Han Solo. Heck, make me Princess Leia if you must, but don't make me some expendable Storm Trooper who doesn't even have a name. From birth we recognize that we have been given a unique identity. While we may have similarities to other people in our looks or our speech, we are totally unique as an individual. Honestly, have you looked at your hands lately? Put the book down and check them out. Look at your thumb (You don't have to put the book down. Just use your other hand). Look at your fingerprint; it is totally unique from any other person. The question is, "Why?" Why haven't we been manufactured in an assembly line fashion? Have you ever watched Science Fiction? Have you noticed that every alien that

> **"I don't care if I'm Luke Skywalker, Obi-Wan Kenobi, Darth Vader, Han Solo. Heck, make me Princess Leia if you must, but don't make me some expendable Storm Trooper who doesn't even have a name."**

lands on Planet Earth is identical to every other member of his species? How do you know whom you're married to if everyone looks the same? Also, have you noticed that everyone dresses the same in the future? Apparently, something catastrophic is going to happen to Calvin Klein, Tommy Hilfiger, and Ralph Lauren, because in every Sci-Fi movie everyone dresses the same: the gray jumpsuit with the big fashionable "V" on the front. Can it get any lamer than that? That's a future that ignores God's creative design. There's something about our uniqueness that glorifies God. It might even seem weird to think that when we are who God created us to be, it makes God happy. Most people don't think about being themselves as something that pleases God. That may be because it doesn't please other people when you act like yourself, so why would it please God (that's a conversation for you and your therapist to have). What I'm saying is this: when I am being the person God created me to be, I glorify Him because my identity reveals God's identity. That is, I reveal God's Person when I'm who God created me to be.

GOD'S FORGOTTEN ATTRIBUTE

Do you know what one of the most overlooked characteristics of God is? I believe it is His creativity. If we were to list some of God's characteristics and attributes, we would speak of His power, wisdom, knowledge, love, patience, and forgiveness. Yet the first verse of the Bible speaks of His creativity.

"In the beginning God created the heavens and the earth." **(Genesis 1:1)**

In fact, the first two chapters of Genesis are all about His creativity. Yet when we get to God creating mankind, it was about more than just creating. It became about revealing Himself. The creation of man was about man being a picture of who God is.

"Then God said, "Let us make man in our image, in our likeness, and let them rule over the fish of the sea and the birds of the air, over the livestock, over all the earth, and over all the creatures that move along the ground." So God created man in his own image, in the image of God he created him; male and female he created them." **(Genesis 1:26-27)**

Even before God created the first man and woman, He already had a plan for them. They were destined to serve God and glorify Him through their unique identities. That's why there's a cultural clash between those that don't know God and followers of Jesus. The world we live in calculates worth based on title, position, and how many people are under you organizationally. I will admit it's hard to break this, because no one wants to be just a Storm Trooper. Instead, they want to be an important person in the story. Before I went into the ministry, I worked for a company which manufactured home accessories. There were seven people who worked in the office and everyone had a title. There were two people who worked in Customer Service, the Manager and the Assistant Manager. Everyone had a title except one person: me. Basically, my job was to do all the stuff everyone else didn't want to. So I gave myself a title to

> **"That's why there's a cultural clash between those that don't know God and followers of Jesus. The world we live in calculates worth based on title, position, and how many people are under you organizationally."**

fit in with everyone else: Jerk Work Manager! Even the CEO knew about my title. Funny enough, he never changed it! Contrast that with God who sees value in all people because they were created in His image. I remember talking to my dad about how good I was with directions. At a ripe 12 years old, I asked him if I could turn that into a career. He said, "Yes, you could be a cab driver." I said, "That's no good." Then he said, "What about driving a fire truck?" I said, "Now you're talking!" That's what the disciples of Jesus were thinking. A title didn't give them value. It was God who gave them value. It was their identity that revealed God's identity and that pleased God. It made them someone God could use to accomplish His purposes in this world. That's why all of them gave themselves the same title. While others called them apostles and they even used that title at times to distinguish themselves, they all gave themselves the name "Doulos." It's a Greek word that we translate "bond-servant," but it really means, "slave." Though the word is translated from Greek, the origin of the word is Hebrew and sheds much light on the title that each of the writers of the New Testament gave themselves.

"If you buy a Hebrew slave, he is to serve for only six years. Set him free in the seventh year, and he will owe you nothing for his freedom. If he was single when he became your slave and then married afterward, only he will go free in the seventh year. But if he was married before he became a slave, then his wife will be freed with him. "If his master gave him a wife while he was a slave, and they had sons or daughters, then the man will be free in the seventh year, but his wife and children will still belong to his master. But the slave may plainly declare, `I love my master, my wife, and my children. I would rather not go free.' If he does this, his master must present him before God. Then his master must take him to the door and publicly pierce his ear with an awl. After that, the slave will belong to his master forever." (Exodus 21:2-6)

You have to understand; this is long before the days of Home Equity Loans and taking out lines of credit. Here's how this situation would work: Let's say you owed someone a lot of money. So much money in fact, that it was too much to pay back. There was no such thing as bankruptcy in those days. Instead, you would become a slave to the person whom you owed the money to and you would work for them for six years. In the seventh year you were free to go and free of your debt. But sometimes, the master would take a liking to the person working for him and he'd give him a girl's phone number or set him up on a date and the slave would get married. The master would treat him better than he was ever treated before. So on the day the servant was to go free, he'd say, "I know I'm free, but I'd like to willingly become a slave of yours forever." Then the master and the slave would go to the gate of the city (like city hall) and there he would declare how good his master has been and reveal his intentions of wanting to remain this man's servant willingly. To display that, the slave would pierce his ear with an awl to symbolize this relationship. Please understand: God was not instituting slavery. Instead, He was regulating it. This was for the purpose of people paying their debts so they could really be free. I've heard of Christian kids that quote this verse to their parents about getting earrings and piercings. "But Mom, it's to prove I love God." Let me just say for the record, "Very slick!"

WRITING CREDENTIALS

Think about any book you've seen. Consider this one. What's the first thing you did after you saw the cover and author's name? You looked at the back to see what makes this person (in this case, me) an expert on the subject they are writing about. Just like you don't take marriage advice from men who have been married multiple times, you don't read books by people who don't know anything about what they are writing about. But these men who wrote the New Testament, you would think they would have put all of their titles, degrees, and positions right up front. Instead, they do the

exact opposite. They simply say, "I'm a willing servant of Jesus."
Let me give you a few examples:

"I, Paul, am a devoted slave of Jesus Christ on assignment..."
(Romans 1:1MSG)

"I, James, am a slave of God and the Master Jesus..."
(James 1:1MSG)

"I, Simon Peter, am a servant and apostle of Jesus Christ."
(2 Peter 1:1MSG)

"I, Jude, am a slave to Jesus Christ and brother to James..."
(Jude 1:1MSG)

What marks your relationship with God? Is it simply words about
giving Jesus your all? Or is it your 'awl,' your pierced life that reflects
His pierced body? Every one of those men we read said the same
thing: "Jesus gave His all for me, the least I can do is give Him my all.
So I'm simply a willing slave of His." I started serving the Lord by
setting up chairs and cutting fruit at 6:30AM on Sundays at church
and I was the happiest guy on the planet. Why? It was my opportunity
to show Jesus how much I loved Him. When I served those that did
or didn't know Jesus I was able to reveal His identity by living out
my identity in Him and the result is people were able to see God through me.

> **What marks your relationship with God? Is it simply words about giving Jesus your all? Or is it your 'awl,' your pierced life that reflects His pierced body?**

me. I see this every week as I walk through my church and I watch
unique people live out their identity and reveal God's identity to me
and to everyone who sees their service to God. Some days it's all

I can do just to keep my composure when I see people serve with joy because Jesus gave His all to them. I pop into our nursery and watch the servants love the kids in their class and change diapers just so parents can hear God's Word taught without the distraction of making sure their young ones aren't killing each other in the aisles or eating weird stuff they find on the floor of the movie theatre we meet in. These kids are never going to thank them when they're older for changing their diaper. But I watch them and they serve with joy because Jesus Christ has invaded their lives, forgiven them of so much, loved them so much, that the only natural response to that is to love and serve the One who forgave and loved that much.

When I was in the tenth grade I had to take English II in Summer School. My teacher's name was Mrs. King. On the first day of class she told us a little bit about herself. She showed us some scars on her arms and she told us the story of how she got them. Her house caught fire one night and she ran through flames to get her daughter. In the process, she was burned badly on her forearm and bicep area. Later her doctor told her she could have cosmetic surgery to cover the scars, but she decided to not have it because she told us, "I'm not ashamed of my scars. It shows how much I love my daughter and there's no reason to cover that up." I learned this lesson that day. I caught a glimpse into what Jesus feels when He sees his scars. He gladly bears the scars that mark His love for you and His service to His Father. So the question is, "Will you be pierced as well? Will you take the name that every Christian before you has taken? Will you bear the name 'Doulos?'" If you do, your identity will reveal His identity...

CHAPTER THREE

Hall Pass

"Sorry folks, the park's closed. The moose outside should have told you."
- Lasky, Walley World Security Guard (National Lampoon's Vacation)

It was the most glorious job! You won't believe me when I tell you what it was, but it was the job that every kid in the eighth grade longed for. In fact, most of us started petitioning for it before the seventh grade let out. I don't know how, perhaps the stars aligned the right way, or God was just being gracious, but somehow I got it. In the eighth grade, I got picked to be on trash duty! That's right, I was your local neighborhood, Catholic schoolboy trash man and I was proud! I know it sounds totally sad, but I think it was one of the happiest days of my young life to be picked for what would later be known as a "Sanitation Engineer" at St. Edward's Catholic School in Brockton, MA. My three friends and I (I still remember them: Marc Celedonio, Joe Brewer, and Mike Newport) were the trash men and it was great. You might be asking why handling the trash of a school that ranged from Kindergarten through eighth grade was so great. The reason is simple. We got to leave class one hour early every day. We got to walk into every class at our leisure, collect the garbage and we got access to the outside while everyone else was stuck in class. Trust me, there's nothing like the sweet smell of freedom when you're locked in class all day. And we flaunted our access. We were the trash men; hear us roar! At times, someone would see us roaming the halls and they would say, "Do you have a hall pass?" We'd just smile and say, "We're on the trash crew." Case closed and access granted! The trash bag was all that people needed to see. Our identity gave us access to wherever we wanted to go.

So much of life is about access and you may have never even realized it. Think about this the next time you drive home from work or the store. You may have to pass through a security gate, that's about access. You may have to put in a password to check your e-mail; that's about access. There's a terrible feeling when you're not allowed somewhere because it's "Authorized Personnel Only." You feel like a loser, unless you're authorized, of course. That must have been what the people of ancient Israel felt like. They were restricted in the one place you would think there would never be restriction: how they could serve God. In Biblical times, the average person was reduced to a spectator because only the priestly tribe of Levi could serve God in the temple. To know what this must have felt like, you've got to put yourself in their sandals. Have you ever wanted to play football during Halftime of the Super Bowl? You've been sitting in front of the TV and you've

> **The lesson is simply that our identity gives us access.**

consumed 30 hot wings, an entire pizza, a bag of chips and a two liter bottle of Diet Coke just to keep it real. You've been watching some great plays, but there's something in you that wants to play too. You know you wouldn't have dropped that pass, thrown that interception, or had that wardrobe malfunction. But what if it was forbidden and illegal for you to even throw a football because only people with the last name Marino or Brady were allowed to? That's how God's people felt when they went to the temple to worship. I'm sure there were moments when the singing, the sacrifices, and the teaching all swept them up and they wanted to express to God their love for Him by participating somehow. But they were prohibited. The reason? They didn't have a hall pass. It's the lesson every Jewish person learned each time he or she came to worship God. It's the lesson that we need to learn if our identity is going to reveal God's identity. It's a lesson that if you embrace it, will change your life. The lesson is simply that our identity gives us access.

SEATING SECTION

So I want to show to show you the levels of access and restriction at the temple. The temple in Jerusalem was an amazing sight to behold. In fact, one ancient writer said, "Whoever has not seen Herod's building has not seen a beautiful building in his life."[2] There were several courts or courtyards for people to worship. The largest was the court of the Gentiles. The open area was on the outer area of the temple and it didn't see much action. These were the bleacher seats. You're in the park, but you're a long way from home plate. It was called the court of the Gentiles because that's as far as Gentiles could go. Jews would spend time there as well, but a Jew could go further while the Gentile had to remain it their section. There was a fence that separated the Gentile area from the next

2 - Chaim Richman The Light of the Temple (Jerusalem, Israel 5758 – 1998) Pg. 8

court and it had an inscription that was written in three languages: "No man of another nation to enter within the fence and enclosure round the temple. And whoever is caught will have himself to blame that his death ensues."[3] The point was, if you aren't Jewish, it's authorized personnel only; no hall pass. But let's say you weren't a Gentile. Instead, you are a devout Jewish woman. If that's the case, then you had a hall pass to get beyond the Gentile court and into the court of the women. Once again, that doesn't mean that only women were there, but that's as far as women could go. If you were a Jewish man, your hall pass extended a bit further and you were allowed to go to the court of the men of Israel. This is where men would bring their sacrifices and where sin would be forgiven. If you were a priest, you go to the next court: the court of the priests. This is where the sacrifices were made and they could enter into the holy place. The holy place was fifteen feet wide and 30 feet long. It is where the golden Menorah and the table of showbread stood. This was symbolic of God's people being always in His presence. The altar of incense was there which spoke of the prayers of God's people always going up to heaven. It was right in front of a large curtain that separated the holy place from a final room that was called, "The Holy of Holies." This was a fifteen-foot by fifteen-foot room wherein was the Ark of the Covenant (If you're ever seen Raiders of the Lost Ark, you've got the right idea) and where God's very presence dwelt. This was no place for tourists or curious onlookers. No one could enter this most sacred of space, save one person and that only one day a year. The high priest alone could enter on the Day of Atonement (Yom Kippur), where he would sprinkle blood on the ark to atone for the sins of the nation. By now, you're reading this wondering, "Why do I need to know this?" It is because it is important for us to know what a privilege it is to

---

be able to serve God in any way. This is because most people spent their entire lives standing on the sidelines or warming the bench, but were never able to get into the game because they didn't have a hall pass. Your nationality, gender, and family of origin determined what kind of seat you were going to get.

JESUS AND CHOCOLATE

Maybe you saw Willy Wonka and the Chocolate Factory or the remake, Charlie and the Chocolate Factory. I'm betting right after you saw it; you were willing to sell a kidney for a milk chocolate bar. I saw it and immediately bought a chocolate bar. I couldn't resist it anymore. I hadn't eaten chocolate in a year until I saw that movie, yet it got the best of me. In the movie, the whole world is going crazy to find one of five golden tickets; hall passes if you will, to experience what they had only been able to watch from a distance. Five lucky children get a hall pass and are able to enter. But what if Willy Wonka created a way for everyone to get a hall pass and experience working in the factory? It would be the answer to the hopes of everyone else that was left on the sidelines with a pile full of wrappers and a face covered in chocolate. In a much greater way, Jesus enabled everyone to get a golden ticket to enter in. He accomplished this by making every believer in Him a priest.

> **But whether you like it or not, you are a priest in God's eyes. God has broken down every barrier that kept us from being able to serve Him.**

That's what was happening in the temple the day He died. Since that day, every person has the opportunity to serve as a priest and experience the joy of serving God and serving God's people.

"Coming to Him as to a living stone, rejected indeed by men, but chosen by God and precious, you also, as living stones, are being built up a spiritual house, a holy priesthood, to offer up spiritual sacrifices acceptable to God through Jesus Christ." **(1 Peter 2:4-5NKJV)**

Now I understand that "Priest" may not be on the top of your career list. You might be thinking that being a priest is right up there with mortician, taxidermist and hearse driver. But whether you like it or not, you are a priest in God's eyes. God has broken down every barrier that kept us from being able to serve Him.

"And Jesus cried out again with a loud voice, and yielded up His spirit. Then, behold, the veil of the temple was torn in two from top to bottom; and the earth quaked, and the rocks were split…" **(Matthew 27:50-51NKJV)**

What did this mean? It meant it was wide open to come to God; everyone has a pass now. This veil that ripped was 60 feet long, 30 feet wide and four inches thick. It is said that it took 300 priests to hang it. The fact that there is no veil means that we have a hall pass; there are no more "Authorized Personnel Only" signs. You might be thinking, "But what about the other courts?" God dealt with those as well. If you're a Gentile, there's no reason to fret, that wall of separation has been dealt with.

"For Christ himself has made peace between us Jews and you Gentiles by making us all one people. He has broken down the wall of hostility that used to separate us." **(Eph. 2:14NKJV)**

But what if I'm a woman? I'm stuck in the court of woman. No, you're not!

"There is neither Jew nor Greek, slave nor free, male nor female, for you are all one in Christ Jesus." **(Galatians 3:28)**

Anyone can serve now and enter in because every believer has a hall pass as a priest. God decided to make you a priest so you have the privilege to do what 1,000's of followers of God only dreamed of doing; serving God in His house. Yet even though we have been given the opportunity, we neglect it. Why? We think watching others serve God is enough. Trust me, it's not. Those who serve at Calvary Fellowship, where I have the privilege of being the Senior Pastor, are the most hardworking, generous, and talented group of people I have ever seen. These people are leading companies, teaching students, managing people, and creating product in the work force. Yet when they gather on a Sunday to serve, all that gets put aside and they assume the title of servant. It is a beautiful thing to see. These people realize God has literally moved heaven and earth so they can serve Him and they aren't about to waste the opportunity to partner with God in His plan to reach the world. That's why when I walk up to them and offer a simple "Thank you" for all they do; do you know what they say? The say, "No. Thank you!" Why would they say that? It is because they realize the amazing privilege it is to partner with God in the redemption of all of mankind. Is there a greater purpose to give your time and energy to? You have the opportunity of a lifetime to partner with Jesus Himself to be part of building what He is building - the local church. Jesus said, "I will build my church." (Matthew 16:18) While I believe that with all my heart, I also subscribe to the Home Depot philosophy as well, "He can do it, but we can help." So do you want a hall pass? You can have one right now and take your post as a priest. All it takes is a willing heart. You've already got someone on the inside who can pull some strings for you. In fact, He's already pulled them. He simply waits for you to respond.

> "You have the opportunity of a lifetime to partner with Jesus Himself to be part of building what He is building - the local church."

My step-dad ran a cold storage facility in Boston for years. He was the man. I would get there and go see him, bypassing all the employees, doors, buzzers, and alarms. I was his son and I could see him whenever I wanted. But there came a time when I wanted to help out and work with him. Most people had to fill out applications, go through a series of interviews, and then maybe they would get the job, But not me. I told him I wanted to help; he pulled a couple of strings, and before you knew it, I was learning to drive a forklift at age twelve. Did any other 12-year-old kids even stand a chance to get hired there? No way! But my relationship gave me access to help him do what he was doing and be part of building what he was building. And I believe that if a kid can find joy in that, imagine the joy we would find in partnering with God to reach this world by building what He is building: the local church.

CHAPTER FOUR

Career Day

*"All in all you're just another brick in the wall. – **Pink Floyd***

When I was a kid, there was only one answer to the question, "What do you want to be when you grow up?". Until I was twelve or thirteen, I would say, "I'm going to pitch for the Red Sox." Then I started pitching and realized that was not going to happen. So I downsized my dream and said I wanted to be a coach for the Red Sox. But most of those guys were old (Like 40, I thought), so I thought my best bet might be to go into broadcasting. In fact, when I started college I was a communications major because I wanted to fulfill that childhood dream, but I couldn't get through all the classes. So I decided I was just going to sell socks for a living! Honestly, I had no clue what I wanted to do with my life. I was 18 and rock star wasn't a possible major, so I took a career aptitude test. If you've never taken one of these, this is like a "What do you want to be now that you're grown up" test. So I answered all the questions and when the results came back, the test said I should become a mathematician! I calculated the test was broken and kept looking for a school that offered "Heavy Metal" in their graduate program.

There is a career you have chosen and other things that you are: Some of you are husbands or wives, moms or dads. If you have kids, at times you feel like a psychiatrist or a chauffeur. But for a Christian, there are certain things we all are. For example, we're called to be a fisher of men.

> **"Most problems in churches take place when people get out of the "service" mentality and into the "serve us" mentality."**

"As Jesus was walking beside the Sea of Galilee, he saw two brothers, Simon called Peter and his brother Andrew. They were casting a net into the lake, for they were fishermen. "Come, follow me," Jesus said, "and I will make you fishers of men." At once they left their nets and followed him." **(Matthew 4:18-20NKJV)**

What you may not be aware of is that there are three other careers God calls us to in our service to Him: Gardener, General Contractor, and Body Builder. Why? Because when I'm doing what I'm supposed to, I have no time to cause problems. Most problems in churches take place when people get out of the "service" mentality and into the "serve us" mentality. It's a fact that when I'm helping to row the boat, I'm too busy to rock it. That's what was happening in a church in the city of Corinth. This group had forgotten why they existed and Paul wanted to refresh their memory. They started thinking that God was there to serve them and their desires, as opposed to what the Scriptures teach that we exist for God's glory and God's pleasure.

A TEAM EFFORT

*"Who then is Paul, and who is Apollos, but ministers through whom you believed, as the Lord gave to each one? I planted, Apollos watered, but God gave the increase. So then neither he who plants is anything, nor he who waters, but God who gives the increase. Now he who plants and he who waters are one, and each one will receive his own reward according to his own labor. For we are God's fellow workers; you are God's field, you are God's building." (**1 Corinthians 3:5-9**)*

Most guys don't think of gardening as a career. Yet every follower of Jesus is a spiritual gardener, tending to the lives of those around us and seeking that they reach their full bloom. For the ladies reading this, when your husband brings you flowers home for no other reason than he loves you, have you ever given a thought to the guy who watered the roses or tended to them? I would be willing to wager that you haven't. You think of your husband for buying them and maybe God for creating such beautiful things. In same way, Paul uses the gardening imagery to show that the key ingredient is God. All of us serve in our own way for the purpose of God being glorified. I truly believe that I get too much credit for what God has done at Calvary Fellowship. There are so many people that do so much to make our services and ministries happen. Yet in the end, God is the One who deserves all of the credit. In baseball, this is called playing for the name on the front of the jersey, not the name on the back. There is a team of people working to bring God's intended result. There is one person who shares the gospel with a friend and sows that initial seed. Then another person expresses God's love through their lifestyle and waters the seed. Then with time another person invites them to church, where hundreds of people serve so that this one person can hear the life-changing Gospel message and they make a decision to come to Christ. That's a team effort where God is glorified. The wonderful part is that He rewards us for all that we do for Him here and eternally…

"According to the grace of God which was given to me, as a wise master builder I have laid the foundation, and another builds on it. But let each one take heed how he builds on it. For no other foundation can anyone lay than that which is laid, which is Jesus Christ. Now if anyone builds on this foundation with gold, silver, precious stones, wood, hay, straw, each one's work will become clear; for the Day will declare it, because it will be revealed by fire; and the fire will test each one's work, of what sort it is. If anyone's work which he has built on it endures, he will receive a reward. If anyone's work is burned, he will suffer loss; but he himself will be saved, yet so as through fire." **(1 Corinthians 3:10-15)**

THE PEOPLE'S COURT

You and I are like general contractors, except we build using our actions, thoughts, and motives. God is the city inspector who is making sure it's up to code. We must understand that all of us are building something. We are building eternal rewards. God is going to judge the buildings that we construct. Now when I use this word "judge" Christians get a little nervous. Allow me to explain this because this is a judgment that every Christian should be looking for ward to. First, we have to understand that when we put our faith in Jesus' finished work on the cross, all of the judgment that I was due, was placed on Jesus. So I don't have to fear standing before God in the sense that I don't know if I will go to heaven or not. Followers of Jesus have this hope, that their salvation is settled because of Jesus' finished work. So this judgment that Paul refers to is not a judgment in reference to salvation. It is a judgment that determines reward.

"For we must all appear before the judgment seat of Christ, that each one may receive what is due him for the things done while in the body, whether good or bad." **(2 Corinthians 5:10)**

The term "Judgment Seat" is the Greek work "Bema" and refers to the ancient Olympic games, where the winners would go to the bema (or judgment seat), not to be condemned or to qualify, but to be rewarded. It was here they received their victory crown, which was a wreath. This is why Paul likens the Christian life to running a race.

"Do you not know that in a race all the runners run, but only one gets the prize? Run in such a way as to get the prize. Everyone who competes in the games goes into strict training. They do it to get a crown that will not last; but we do it to get a crown that will last forever."
(1 Corinthians 9:24-25)

Here's what we're building: The day will come when we stand before God. At that time, we are going to be rewarded for what we did with what God gave us. Just like military officers display rank on their chests, the crown shows rank. According to 1 Corinthians 3:10-15, all of our works are going to be tested by fire.

What does fire do? It burns away things like wood, hay, and straw, yet it purifies gold, silver, and precious stones. Those things that we did for God's glory will withstand the test and remain, the things that perhaps had impure motives, will burn away. I believe this will determine what our responsibilities will be in the eternal kingdom of God. Do you remember the parable Jesus told in Matthew 25 about three men who were given talents? One is given five talents, another is given two talents, and the last is given one. I used to feel bad for the guy who was given one until I researched it and discovered that one talent was worth over $5 million. The purpose of the parable is to show us that what we do with what God has given us will result in eternal blessing later.

"His lord said to him, "Well done, good and faithful servant; you were faithful over a few things, I will make you ruler over many things. Enter into the joy of your lord." **(Matthew 25:21)**

WHAT A PONCHO CAN TEACH US ABOUT ETERNITY

The responsibilities we will have eternally are dependent on what we do now. You might say, "Well, I'm not into crowns. I'll be happy just being there." You may say that now, but you won't then. In 1992, I went to the one and only football game I have ever gone to. I love football; I just believe that watching it at my house in HD is much better than going to the stadium. It was the AFC East divisional playoff game between the Dolphins and the Chargers. The sky looked a little dark and they were selling ponchos outside.

> **"God gives us the opportunity to use our current situation to affect our eternal responsibilities."**

I didn't buy one because I thought, "Who needs that? If it rains it rains." Let me say, it rained. And then it rained some more. I mean it poured nonstop for the entire first half of the game. I went inside to buy a poncho but by then the price had doubled and they were sold out. I then regretted not using my opportunity to influence my future situation. I know comparing heaven to a rainy football game isn't the best illustration, but the point is that God gives us the opportunity to use our current situation to affect our eternal responsibilities. That's why we need to use our time, our talents, and our treasure wisely. This way, we can build a structure that passes the refiner's fire and is blessed eternally.

"Do you not know that you are the temple of God and that the Spirit of God dwells in you? If anyone defiles the temple of God, God will destroy him. For the temple of God is holy, which temple you are. Let no one deceive himself. If anyone among you seems to be wise in this age, let him become a fool that he may become wise. For the wisdom of this world is foolishness with God. For it is written, "He catches the wise in their own craftiness"; and again, "The LORD knows the thoughts of the wise, that they are futile." Therefore let no one boast in men. For all things are

yours: whether Paul or Apollos or Cephas, or the world or life or death, or
things present or things to come—all are yours. And you are Christ's, and
*Christ is God's." **(1 Corinthians 3:16-23)***

FUN HOUSE MIRROR

Those that know me are well aware that I don't look like a body
builder, but I am one nonetheless. You may look in the mirror and
see a keg where a six-pack should be, but you are a body builder
as well. You're not one like Governor Arnold, you're a different
type. You're someone that builds the body of Christ. You are God's
temple, His holy dwelling place. According to God, you and I
together are a building that houses the Holy Spirit.

"And now God is building you, as living stones, into his spiritual temple.
What's more, you are God's holy priests, who offer the spiritual sacrifices
*that please him because of Jesus Christ." **(1 Peter 2:5)***

We know there are different types of homes. There's the kind
of homes that are in your neighborhood, there's the homes that
aren't so nice, and then there's the MTV Cribs type of homes. In
1 Corinthians 3:16, the word used for building isn't the normal
Greek word you would use for your average building. It's the Greek
Word "Naos", which refers to the Holy of Holies, where the glory
of God dwelt (we talked about that in the last chapter). That's
why Paul ends this section saying that division is silly because it's
unnecessary. We are all after the same goal. I remember visiting my
former town home when it was being built. I remember seeing the
foundation being laid, the walls get put up, the roof go on. What
blew me away was that all of this work was taking place for me. It
wasn't about one brick over another; they were all playing their
part for the greater purpose of the one who was going to live there.
That's what we are all doing. We are each a brick in God's building.
We are all a part of God's awesome plan. For His glory, not ours...

CHAPTER FIVE

Frequentky Asked Questions About Serving

1. Who should serve?

I am a firm believer that all Christians should serve. The reason being is that the Bible teaches we are a body and every part of the body has a specific function (1 Cor. 12). There's no part of the human body that's just along for the ride. Instead, health is all the parts of the body working as they should. In the church, the same holds true. Every person who is part of the body of Christ has a vital role to play and when we fulfill that role, the Church is healthier.

2. What's the best place for me to discover my gifts?

Honestly, the best place to discover your gifts is to simply start doing something. I've always said that a moving car is easier to steer.

If you start serving in an area of the church and you don't like it, move to another area. Before long, you'll find a place you love to serve, where your gifts match your passion.

3. What should be my motivation for serving?

The apostle Paul wrote, "If I speak in the tongues of men and of angels, but have not love, I am only a resounding gong or a clanging cymbal. If I have the gift of prophecy and can fathom all mysteries and all knowledge, and if I have a faith that can move mountains, but have not love, I am nothing. If I give all I possess to the poor and surrender my body to the flames, but have not love, I gain nothing." (1 Corinthians 13:1-3) Love is the only true motivation for service that will last. There are things we do because they are fun. There are things we do because they seem like the right thing to do, but service that is motivated by love for Jesus is the only service that lasts.

4. What do I do if I feel burnt out?

There's a difference between being tired and getting burnt out. Being tired from a day of service to the Lord is a great feeling. It's knowing that you expended all your energy in serving God's people. Burn out comes from continuous service in an area that is not our gifting. What prevents burnout is serving in a rhythm that allows for breaks and rest. Also, people who are doing what they love are far less likely to suffer burnout. Here's the bottom line: serve with all your heart in an area of ministry you love. Take breaks to get refueled and recharged and you're no likely to suffer burnout.

5. I serve in organizations outside the church. Do I really need to serve inside the church as well?

If you are part of a local church, you should have opportunity to give and receive. We receive through teaching, public worship and personal ministry. We give through tithes, offerings, and service. The body of Christ needs every part working to be healthy. In many churches, few people do the work of many. Healthy churches are filled with healthy Christians who all do the ministry God has called them to do and experience the rewards of service.

6. What should I do if I'm too busy to serve?

People give their time to what's important. If you asked me to take on 20 extra hours of responsibility for a project, I would likely say no citing my schedule. Yet every year I watch the World Series, which is at least a 20 hour commitment. How am I able to accommodate it into my schedule? Commitment. If you're too busy to serve, here's my honest counsel to you: find the time. You will be better off spiritually, but the Body of Christ will be healthier as well.

7. Why is serving so important to my growth as a Christian?

The Christian life is not a spectator sport. It's where we partner with God in His redemptive mission. Serving is where we play our part in building up His Church. When a believer doesn't serve, they leave so much undone that God wants to do in their lives. When a Christian serves, He pours himself out and allows God to fill him up again. When I don't serve, I get stuck and God can't pour into me any more until I pour myself out again. That's why the most mature Christians are those who continually give of themselves. That way, God entrusts them with more and they are given greater Kingdom responsibility.

CONCLUSION
The Conclusion of the Matter

Two decisions have affected my life most as a follower of Jesus. The first was when I decided to start honoring God with my finances. I heard a Pastor speak boldly from God's Word is regards to tithing and I decided to take God at His Word and obey. Years have past and I can happily report that God has been faithful to me; more faithful than I probably deserve. The second decision was the choice to roll up my sleeves and get involved in the church that I called home. I know I wasn't solving all of the world's problems by setting up chairs early on Sunday mornings, but that decision that was my first step is learning to beyond myself.

So here's my final challenge to you: serve! Don't let the reading of this book be merely educational. Instead, allow it to be a living push to get you going in the right direction. Find a place of service and honor God with the gifts and talents He has given to you. Jesus modeled servanthood for us and we are most like Jesus when we are doing what He did. So serve in your local church. Pick up a bucket like Jesus in John 13 and find the fulfillment you've been looking for. Fulfillment is never found when I'm living for myself. It's found in the service of our King.

I'll tell you a secret: the person who is willing to pick up a bucket and serve is the kind of person God can use to do great things for His Kingdom. Do you want to be great? Serve. Do you want to be influential for the Kingdom of God? Serve. Do you want to model Jesus for your kids? Serve. Do you want to be more like Jesus? Serve. Pick up the bucket. Everything you've been looking for is there.

NOTES

www.ingramcontent.com/pod-product-compliance
Lightning Source LLC
Chambersburg PA
CBHW060620030426
42337CB00018B/3128